An Eye on Spiders

Water Spiders

by Jenna Lee Gleisner

Bullfrog Books

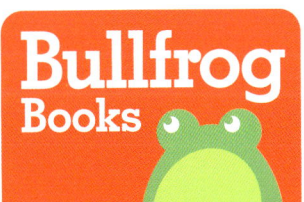

Ideas for Parents and Teachers

Bullfrog Books let children practice reading informational text at the earliest reading levels. Repetition, familiar words, and photo labels support early readers.

Before Reading
- Discuss the cover photo. What does it tell them?
- Look at the picture glossary together. Read and discuss the words.

Read the Book
- "Walk" through the book and look at the photos. Let the child ask questions. Point out the photo labels.
- Read the book to the child, or have him or her read independently.

After Reading
- Prompt the child to think more. Ask: Water spiders are the only spiders in the world that spend their entire lives underwater. What other animals do you know that live their entire lives underwater?

Bullfrog Books are published by Jump!
5357 Penn Avenue South
Minneapolis, MN 55419
www.jumplibrary.com

Copyright © 2019 Jump! International copyright reserved in all countries. No part of this book may be reproduced in any form without written permission from the publisher.

Library of Congress Cataloging-in-Publication Data

Names: Gleisner, Jenna Lee, author.
Title: Water spiders / by Jenna Lee Gleisner.
Description: Minneapolis, MN : Jump!, Inc., [2018]
Series: Bullfrog books. An eye on spiders
"Bullfrog Books are published by Jump!"
Audience: Ages 5–8. | Audience: K to grade 3.
Includes bibliographical references and index.
Identifiers: LCCN 2017041710 (print)
LCCN 2017041198 (ebook)
ISBN 9781624967993 (ebook)
ISBN 9781624967986 (hardcover : alk. paper)
Subjects: LCSH: Water spider—Juvenile literature.
Spiders—Juvenile literature.
Classification: LCC QL458.42.A75 (print)
LCC QL458.42.A75 G54 2018 (ebook) | DDC 595.4/4—dc23
LC record available at https://lccn.loc.gov/2017041710

Editor: Kristine Spanier
Book Designer: Molly Ballanger

Photo Credits: Sergey Peterman/Shutterstock, cover (top); MYN/Niall Benvie/Nature Picture Library, cover (bottom), 1; Hakan Soderholm/Alamy, 3, 6–7, 23tr; Stephen Dalton/Minden Pictures/Getty, 4, 11, 17, 20–21; Gerhard Schulz/Getty, 5, 23tl; Heidi & Hans-Juergen Koch/Minden Pictures/Getty, 8–9; Robert F. Sisson/Getty, 10, 12–13; John A. L. Cooke/Animals Animals, 14–15, 23br; NHPA/Superstock, 16, 23bl; AnnaTamila/Shutterstock, 18–19; Scenics & Science/Alamy, 22; Chris Martin Bahr/Biosphoto, 24.

Printed in the United States of America at Corporate Graphics in North Mankato, Minnesota.

3 5944 00141 1006

Table of Contents

Underwater Home	4
Where in the World?	22
Picture Glossary	23
Index	24
To Learn More	24

Underwater Home

In a pond, a spider builds a home.

diving bell

It is not a web.
What is it?
A diving bell!

6

What spider lives here?

A water spider.

It lives its whole life underwater!

How?

Tiny hairs.

Its body is covered in them.

hairs

9

He goes to the top.

Air stays in his hairs.

He fills the bell with the air bubbles.

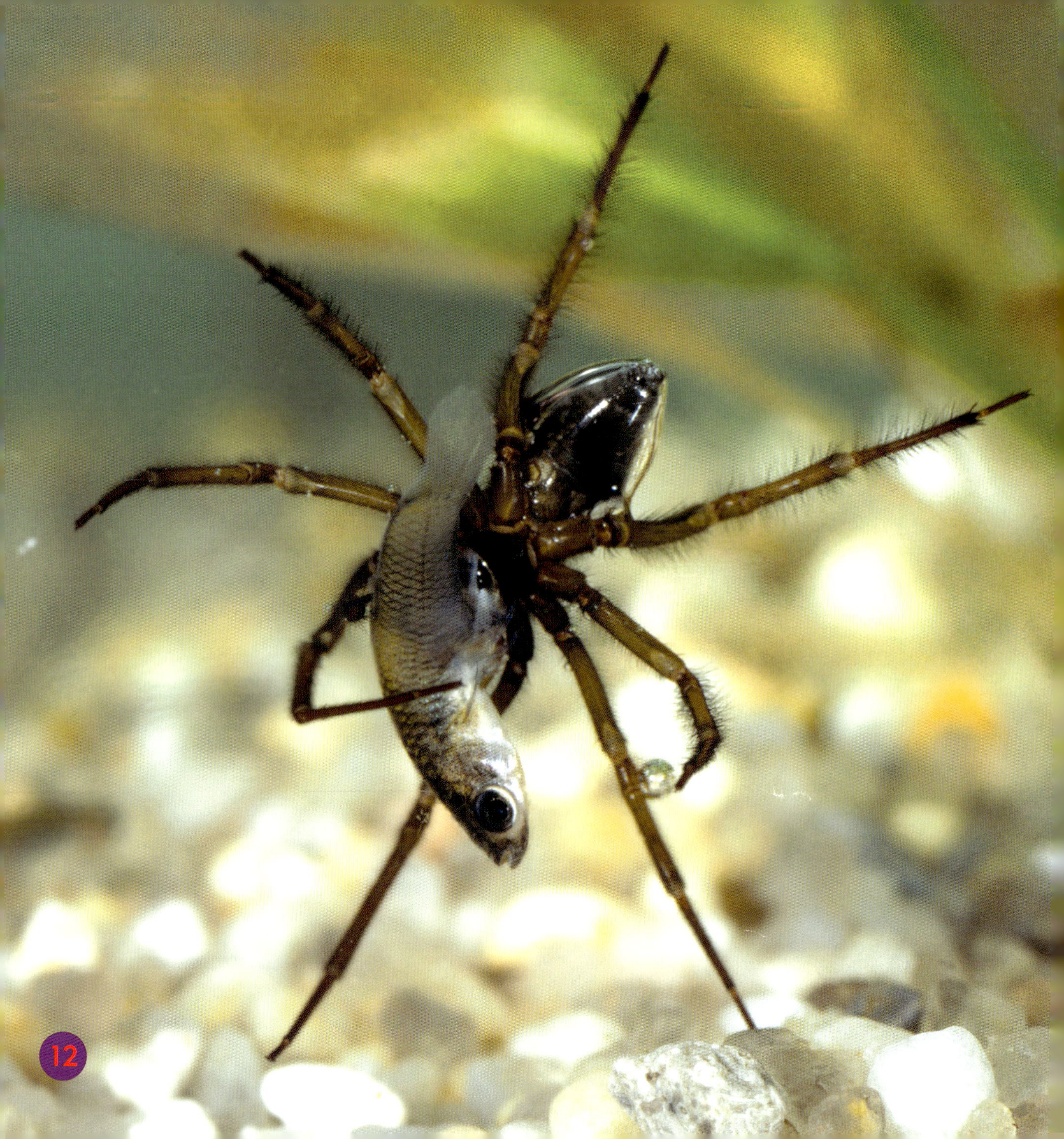

Males hunt outside the bell.

Females stay in.

Prey comes close.

They catch it!

prey

See the egg sac?

Females lay eggs in the bell.

They hatch after a few weeks.

egg sac

They make their own bells.

Winter is coming.

Brr!

The spider will hibernate.

19

20

He goes deeper.

He builds a new bell.

It is stronger.

He will come
out in spring.

Where in the World?

Water spiders live in ponds, shallow lakes, and slow-moving streams. They can be found throughout Northern and Central Europe, Siberia, Northern Asia, and Britain.

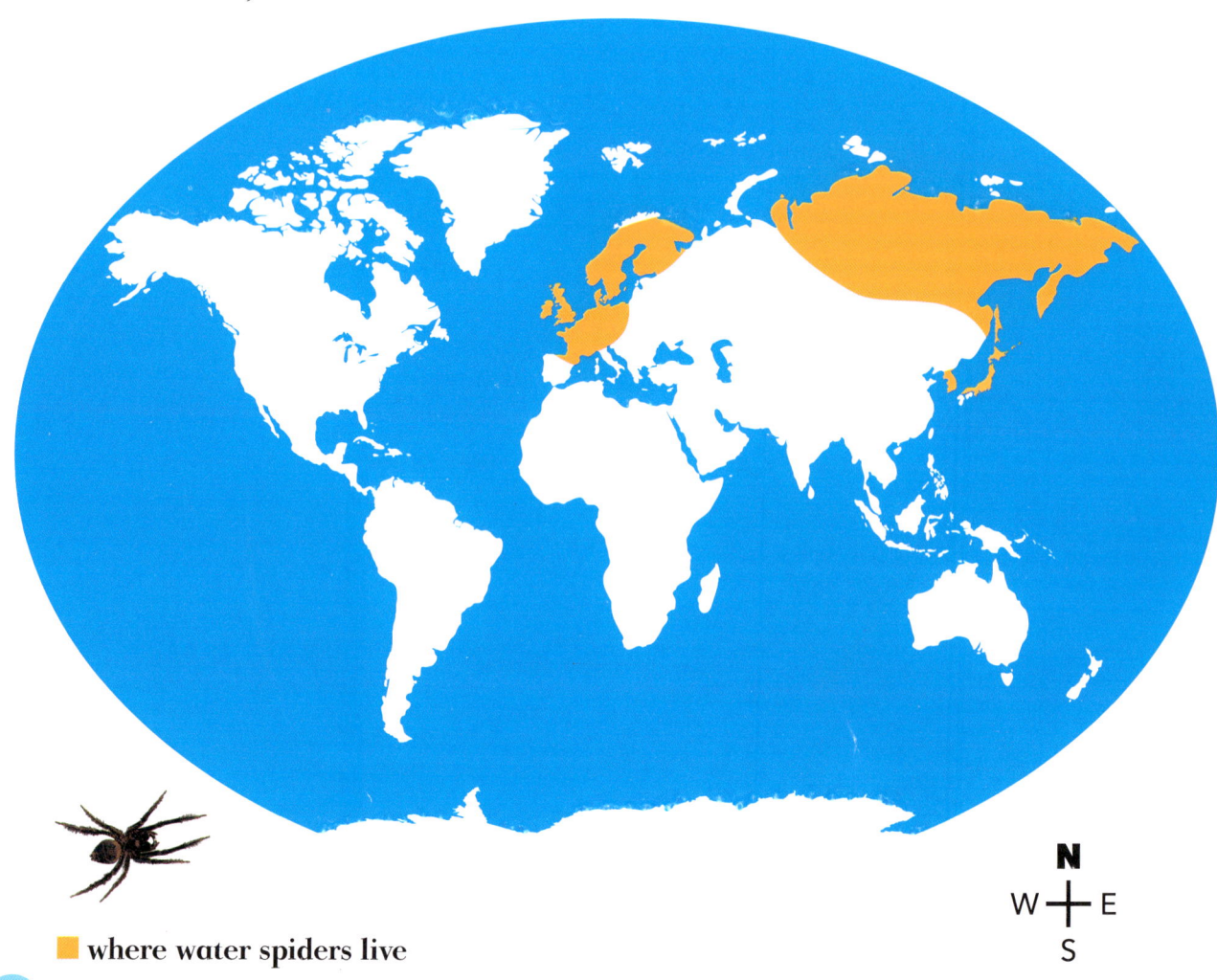

■ where water spiders live

Picture Glossary

diving bell
An underwater chamber open on the bottom but filled with air for divers to go in.

hibernate
To sleep through the winter to survive cold temperatures.

egg sac
A protective pouch in which a female spider puts her eggs.

prey
An animal that is hunted by another animal for food.

Index

air 10, 11
bell 5, 11, 13, 16, 17, 21
body 8
eggs 16
egg sac 16
hairs 8, 10
hatch 16
hibernate 18
home 4
hunt 13
pond 4
prey 14

To Learn More

Learning more is as easy as 1, 2, 3.
1) Go to www.factsurfer.com
2) Enter "waterspiders" into the search box.
3) Click the "Surf" button to see a list of websites.

With factsurfer.com, finding more information is just a click away.

North Smithfield Public Library

P Creepy Crawly 595.44 Gle
Gleisner, Jenna Lee, author
Water spiders

35944001411006

9/2018 P 18
Creepy
Crawly
595.44
Gle